The Sparrow Finds Her Home: A Journey to Find the True Self

About the Author

Doris J. Mical is a Sister of St Joseph of Peace. She has worked in a variety of ministries in various capacities, including teaching, Parish Religious Education Director, Novice Director, and Founder and Director of Spirit Center, a place of prayer, hospitality, and healing for women.

As a Pastoral Counselor she has worked in several settings in both group and private practice. She is also a private Spiritual Director and a Retreat Director. In addition, she is presently working as a Resident Advocate in a home for the aged.

Doris is also the mother of Joe Mical, Scott Mical and Sean Mical and the grandmother of Allyson Mical, Makenzie Mical, and Jayden Mical.

About the Cover Artist

The cover of the sparrow and the rainbow was painted for Doris' birthday by Makenzie Mical, her eleven-year-old granddaughter.

The Sparrow Finds Her Home:
A Journey to Find the True Self

Doris J. Mical, CSJP

Kenmare Press
2019

Copyright © 2019 by Doris J. Mical, CSJP

All rights reserved. This book or any portion thereof may not be reproduced or used in any manner whatsoever without the express written permission of the publisher except for the use of brief quotations in a book review or scholarly journal.

First Printing: 2019

ISBN: 978-0-359-80045-2

e-ISBN: 978-0-359-80052-0

Library of Congress Control Number: 2019910136

Kenmare Press
An imprint of the Sisters of St. Joseph of Peace
399 Hudson Terrace
Englewood Cliffs, New Jersey 07632

www.csjp.org

This book is dedicated to the memory of my son Sean Seton Mical, whose life on earth was much too brief but whose spirit continues to guide and protect me.

Contents

Acknowledgements ix
Introduction 1
Chapter 1: The Bird Feeders 5
Chapter 2: Eagle/Sparrow Metaphor 7
Chapter 3: The Birth of the Eagle 9
Chapter 4: Turbulent Weather 17
Chapter 5: Homing Time For The Sparrow 21
Chapter 6: The Eagle Soars 25
Chapter 7: Flying Full Circle 33
Chapter 8: Eagle Eyed 37
Chapter 9: The Sparrow's Molting Instinct 41
Chapter 10: Bird Song 45
Chapter 11: The Lark At Heaven's Gate 51
Chapter 12: A Bird's Eye View 53
References 55

Acknowledgements

This book would not exist without the support of so many who helped to shape my life. I am first grateful to God who provided the inspiration and gift that made it possible for me to recognize my desire to share the lessons that I have learned with others.

I am grateful to:

my Religious Congregation, The Sisters of St Joseph of Peace, for the gift of shared history and for the many opportunities for growth and community. Your generosity has been without measure.

my parents and siblings who shared the early years with me – in whose footsteps I walked and who played no small part in my "becoming."

my immediate family, my sons and my grandchildren, your presence in my life is beyond words to express. You challenge me, you support me, and you love me – your presence is pure gift.

Sister Liz Sweeney, SSJ, whose wisdom and support were invaluable to me in my discernment and spiritual growth. Thank you for being with me during difficult times of choice and challenge.

Sister Clare D'Auria, OSF, I will forever be grateful for your invaluable gifts of insight and wisdom, as I pursued the writing of this book. Thank you for accompanying me as I struggled to understand the depth of the transformative meaning of the eagle and the sparrow in my journey toward self-knowledge.

Edwina Gateley for permission to use her poem "Let Your God Love You" and to the Carmelite Sisters of the Mother of God, for permission to use "The Legend of the Sparrow (For a child who dreams of sainthood)" by Jessica Powers.

Sister Susan Francois, CSJP, Jan Linley, and Cristina Turino, for contributing their expertise and professional experience to the printing of this book.

Fran McInerney, friend and colleague, who in times of doubt, as I pursued this endeavor, provided much needed support when "the going got tough."

Introduction

Storytelling is the most personal, spontaneous, and basic way of naming our experiences. It requires us to explore the memories and images that link our faith stories with our life experiences. In each of us there is a craving to live authentically, to speak and to act according to what is genuinely me.

How do we enter into and maintain a relationship with God that has the potential for the revelation of God's Self and the personal self? I believe that it begins with the willingness to "come as we are" to God. It presupposes the desire to accept and to embrace within ourselves all that it is to be human – the darkness and the light, the successes and the failures, the sinfulness and the virtues. The challenge is to find a way in which all of life's realities become pathways of God's grace rather than obstacles to it. It demands an ongoing quest for self-knowledge and self-acceptance.

Gradually I began to see my spiritual journey's dependence on the narrative of my daily life as it unfolded. The metaphors that I used to define my journey began to emerge as I began to remember and articulate the pattern that has most clearly impacted my life choices.

So often what seems random and meaningless at first, actually turns out to be very important. It was during one of those times that I heard myself responding to a comment from my spiritual director, by sharing that, "the sparrow has found her home." I had no idea where that came from – it was truly spontaneous and unplanned. I don't remember that I even thought much about it after that. It was only after I was encouraged to write a book, by some of the wisdom people in my life, that the thought began to take on a life of its own.

As I began to reflect on the deeper meaning of those words several questions emerged:

"Where was the sparrow before she found her home? Who was she before that? What might have been the obstacles and detours that impacted her desire to be other than who she was?

My search for answers to these three questions led to the metaphor of the sparrow and the eagle. In retrospect the eagle seemed to represent the choices that I made in life that did not support my true self. The sparrow represented the place where I felt at home and truly myself. I began to understand more fully the physical, emotional, and spiritual impact that the events of my life had on me – the ways in which they changed and transformed me, sometimes for better, sometimes for worse, but always significantly.

As I continued to explore my story, I was able to experience a congruity in the belief that all that happens to us has meaning and purpose. Whatever the plot of our stories, their purpose is to help us to connect inwardly to the movement of God's Spirit in order to live life with greater awareness and authenticity.

There is a Sufi legend about some anxious fish who kept swimming about looking for the sea. A wise fish happened to see them and suggested that if they would stop darting around so anxiously, they would be able to see that the sea was all around them. They needed to look no further than where they were.

This story reminds me that we are surrounded by an abundance of God's grace and by the mystery of God's Self. The world we live in pulsates with God's presence. What God wants most is for us to become our best selves. Everything that we will need in order to do that is already given. All that we must do is to appreciate and accept the invitation to "come as we are." The metaphor of the eagle and the sparrow was a grace that helped me to move with greater clarity and conviction into a journey that will take a lifetime.

The Legend of the Sparrow
(For a child who dreams of sainthood)

There was a sparrow who dreamed to fly
into the sun.
Oh, how the birds of air set up a cry
at such imprudence in a little one
When even eagles dared not venture near
the burning stratosphere.

"She will come down within a mile or two,"
they prophesied with dread.
It was, of course, so pitifully true.
Scarce half-way up the mountain overhead
she crashed into her feathers, as they said.

But when her wings healed, up she shot again
and sought a further bough.
She was more humble and more cautious now,
after a brief novitiate of pain.

Three times she rose; twice the wind brought her down,
once her own weariness.
At last she clutched a branch in her distress
and cried, "How can I ever hope to rest
in the sun's downy nest?
I faint; I fall whatever way I go!"

But then she turned and saw the home she left
unnumbered miles below,
while just beyond her lay the mountain top,
a kerchiefed head of snow.

Nobody told her and she never guessed
that earth's last height was all that she need seek.

All winds blow upward from the mountain peak
and there the sun has such magnetic rays
that in one moment she was lifted up
into his tender blaze.

Down in the valley there was such a stir:
A sparrow reached the sun!
Why had the wind and weather favored her?
What had she ever done?
Yet since they must, they spoke the praising word,
Measured her flight and paused to gasp afresh.
What was she really but a little bird,
all feather and no flesh?

Only the sun knew, and the moving air
the miracle thereof:
a bird that wings itself with resolute love
can travel anywhere.

    Jessica Powers (1946)

1
The Bird Feeders

"His eye is on the sparrow, and I know He watches me."

   Civilla Durfee Martin

"Use what talents you possess: the woods would be very silent
    if no birds sang there except those that sang the best."

I realized some time ago that one of the gifts that I have been given is that of writing. I am remembering that even in school it was something that came easily to me. A number of times I wrote essays that were sent by my teachers to contests for high school students. Of course, I was always delighted if I won but even, if not, I found the writing gratifying. I read somewhere recently that the person that we are meant to be is hidden in the depths of the gifts that we have been given. For whatever reason, as life began to twist and turn, I ignored this gift for a long time. It was at a weekend retreat at our community retreat house that I rediscovered it. We were invited by our retreat facilitator to take a walk on the grounds of the retreat house which faces the ocean and to create a metaphor about creation. I surprised myself as I wrote:

"My God is like the ocean,
He continually covers the beaches of my heart
with his tenacious love for me."

It certainly isn't a sign of brilliance, but it reawakened in me a desire to revisit that part of myself. Since then, I frequently write reflections and poems during my retreats and in my journal writings. With the help of my spiritual director, they have become an integral part of my reflection and, as such, a powerful tool for knowing myself and my relationship with God.

Recently I visited with my brother Bill and his wife Doreen in their home in Naples, Florida. I stayed with them for four days and then went to Lakewood, Florida to spend four days with Sister Janet Richardson, CSJP and Sister Rosalie McQuaide, CSJP. As Sister Janet is often known to say, a "marvelous" time was had by all. Unaware that I was secretly considering the possibility of writing a memoir, my brother Bill suggested that I write a book and while visiting with Sister Janet, she also made the same suggestion. This has been suggested to me many times before, including by other CSJP Sisters and my spiritual director. Of course, in Sister Janet's well known and loving way she insisted that I begin today, Friday, at 10:00 a.m. and continue to write every day at the same time, for one hour when possible. I am inserting the last phrase "when possible." Janet would say that it's a choice and always possible. I am encouraged by her promise of prayer for this intention.

2
Eagle/Sparrow Metaphor

So here we go! At this point I have no idea where this will take me. However, I do trust the evidence of the past that I will be guided by God's Spirit as I have been always in the past. I am also somewhat intrigued by the excitement that I am now feeling in my body for this project. I am surprised by that!

The best place to start might be to explain why I chose this title, "The Sparrow Has Found Her Home" for this book. As I have matured by grace and wisdom over many years, I have learned a number of important things about myself. One of the most important, I believe, is that I have carried a heavy burden in my desire to be an "eagle" in this world. I should explain that I am considering "eagle" as a metaphor for greatness/distinguishable and "sparrow" as a metaphor for average/indistinguishable. I wanted to do great things. Now there's nothing wrong with the desire to do great things, but there is something very wrong with the innate and mostly unconscious desire, at least at first, to be known and seen as great.

First, of course, I have no control over how others see me. Secondly, I, like others, have been given certain gifts that are derived from a unique and somewhat limited gene pool. So, the possibilities for greatness are not particularly within my control. Thirdly, and most importantly, my definition of greatness was definitely lacking.

In an effort to understand more fully this metaphor of the eagle and the sparrow, I have tried to learn more about their characteristics. Eagles are certainly impressive and powerful looking creatures. Sparrows not so much. It has been said that the remarkable thing about sparrows is how unimpressive they are. Because the eagle flies higher than any other bird he is considered chief of all flying creatures. A single sparrow on its own would probably escape notice, while an eagle is often met with the delightful cries of onlookers. Perhaps, for now, that is enough of a metaphor to make my point.

3
The Birth of the Eagle

Every family has its own challenges, its secrets, its failings and its shadows. With that in mind, I think that it might be helpful to share how I got to where I am now. As we begin to understand more clearly our personal history, we can begin to heal our wounds and name our blessings.

I am the oldest of five children. We were certainly well taken care of physically, but circumstances in the family system made emotional and even psychological development more difficult. I have often referred to this deterrent as a demon. Alcoholism has been a generational blip in many families. My grandfather, my father, and other members of my family have suffered, and still suffer, the debilitating consequences of its venom. Sadly, enough it is one of the major contributors to poor self-images, guilt, shame, and efforts at over-achievement in most who are touched by its sting.

As I mentioned, I grew up the oldest of five children. The first child in a challenged family is often referred to as "the hero child." I would say that I fit that label very well – not "hero" because most "favored" but because from the time I can remember I decided that the way for me to be visible was to excel. I also thought that in doing so I could somehow control the tension in my family. When I was doing something praise-worthy I created a distraction in the family system. I believe that this was the beginning of the "eagle complex."

My first memory as a child is of being carried on the shoulders of my dad as we left the hospital after I had my tonsils removed. I must have been two or three years old at the time. I am not quite sure why that is my earliest memory – unless it's because it was an unusual thing for my dad to do. He wasn't that kind of a physical dad. He was usually rather laid back and quiet – unless, of course he was drinking. For some reason I have attached that possibility to my memory.

My next memories of him in early childhood are not very pleasant. They are of much drama and childhood fears connected with his drinking. When I was five years old, he went into the Navy. I have been told that he was given the choice to go into the Navy or to deal with the legal consequences of his addiction. He chose the Navy. This was during World War II, and evidently, it was a choice that he later regretted.

My grandmother, my dad's mom, came to live with us at the time. My mother went to work and my grandmother took care of us. My mother and my grandmother had a difficult time getting along.

My dad was the only child of an Irish immigrant mother and an Irish immigrant father. My paternal grandfather left a family in Ireland, and he and my grandmother, in her mid-forties, had one son. As far as we know, they were never married. When my dad was twelve years old, his father fell down the stairs in a drunken stupor and died. Age, and the experience of my own propensity for weakness, have made me understand with greater empathy the difficulties of my father's journey, given the absence in his young life of any parental support. I wonder how different life might have been for him if he had been given half a chance.

A widowed Irish immigrant mother was not about to give up her only son to another woman without a fight, even when it became apparent that he had fathered a child. In spite of the ensuing struggle, my parents were married in the rectory of the nearby Catholic Church. My mother was barely eighteen, and my father was twenty. They had been next-door neighbors all of their lives. I was born seven months later. I don't think that my grandmother ever forgave my mother for "taking her son away from her." I was told much later that she had put an Irish curse on their unborn child. Perhaps as a result of that, I never felt very close to my grandmother. I always felt that she favored my brother and sister. The last time that I saw her was when I was a novice and she was dying. I wondered if she remembered the curse. I hoped not.

My sister Frances was born ten and a half months after me. She was named after my mother. When I asked mom, why, as the oldest daughter, I wasn't named after her, she said that I was named after a favorite doll that she had as a child. I accepted that but now realize that since my grandmother was also named Frances, it would not have been a good idea to name me Frances given their relationship at the time of my birth.

I have always had strong loving feelings toward my mother. She had a very difficult life. Her mother died when she was five years old. She had several siblings, but they were much older than she. After my maternal grandmother died, my grandfather hired a housekeeper, who had three husbands precede her in death. Evidently my grandfather was at a loss as to how to earn a living and take care of this young child. The story is that after he became dependent on the help of this housekeeper, she threatened to quit if he didn't marry her. And he eventually did. There are some horrific stories of her jealousy toward my mother, the young child. One of them is that without his knowledge or permission she made arrangements to put her in a Children's Home. He resisted, and we are told that he threatened to send his housekeeper/wife away instead. The abuse continued in more subtle ways throughout her childhood.

As a result, my mother was ill-prepared to have two children within ten and a half months. She was very protective of us, and I believe that she did the best that she could. She never had a role model for mothering and at times needed a mother herself. Her way of getting that was often to play the victim. She also had a husband who, at that time, was more of a burden than a partner. All of that created a broken family system. However, in spite of her limitations, I credit her with keeping it together. Somehow, she even found the strength to insist, or should I say demand, for the most part, that my father work to support his family. Even when he was in the Navy, his income was sent to her.

In spite of that, there were often financial struggles. My mother always wanted us to have the things that our peers had. Providing that, however, meant creating a lot of credit debt. She did her best to keep up with it, but sometimes it was overextended. I remember one particular Easter when she took my sister and me to one of the stores that she frequented, and she was told that she could not buy our Easter outfits on credit. She cried all of the way home. The next day, Easter Sunday, it rained all day, and no one wore their Easter outfits.

As I mentioned before, my sister Frances was born ten and a half months after me. Some people refer to this as Irish twins. Frances was a beautiful child. She had big dimples and naturally curly hair. She received a lot of attention because of her striking looks. My mother was especially proud of her and I believe liked the attention that she received as the mother of this child. At ten and a half months old, there was a new baby on my mother's lap, and I had to be "the big girl." This certainly could have been an early contributor to the "eagle complex."

I really don't know if I heard this myself or if I was told it, but my mother once commented, "Frances has the beauty and Doris has the brains." Guess what? At that time, I didn't hear that as a compliment. I wanted the attention that Frances received because of her beauty.

One striking example of my childhood jealousy happened when Frances was in the kindergarten and I was in the first grade. Both grades were in the same classroom. Every year in May, a child in that classroom was chosen to crown the statue of the Blessed Virgin Mary. It was a big deal. She wore a wedding gown which had been made in the size of the young child. After the other children in the class had processed into the Church, she processed alone up to the statue and was lifted up to put the crown on the statue of Mary.

The child was chosen by lottery. The names of the girls were put into a box and the name of the lucky child was pulled out. Frances was the child whose name was selected. Evidently, I was devastated and was certain that they chose her because she was so beautiful.

Although Frances and I certainly loved each other, we were not close friends. For a while we went to the same school but when the family moved, we went to different schools and had different friends. We seemed to handle the dysfunction in the family differently. It seems to me that she pretty much ignored it, and I definitely internalized it but did everything that I could to hide it and pretend that it didn't exist. I became the bearer of the "big secret." My friends never knew anything intimate about my family. I know now that I carried the shame for the family. I also know that it is not unusual for the oldest in an alcoholic family to do that. I had some unconscious belief that if I could make my parents proud of me, by what I achieved, things would change. I became the overachiever – sowing the seeds of the "eagle complex."

My mother was pregnant with my brother Billy when my father went into the Navy. He was named after my father and as the first son he was adored by all, especially by my paternal grandmother. I remember him as a very sweet and quiet child. We have a picture of him at about two years old wearing a genuine sailor suit. I don't remember very much about those years when my father was in the Navy. I was about five years old at the time. I do know that I made my First Communion while he was still in the Navy, because there is a picture of me and my mother sitting on a large rock and I was all dressed up in my white dress and veil.

Although Billy was the third child, he always seemed like the "rock" in the family. As a child he protected himself from much of the drama by removing himself from it. I believe that my mother bestowed on him, in her mind anyway, the strength that was absent in my father. I wonder how that affected him. I do think that early on, perhaps in childhood, he determined that in the future his life would be different and that gave him the strength to not internalize the drama. He has been very successful and has always been a generous source of support for all of us.

Arlene was the fourth child and the youngest for thirteen years. She was a very pretty child with long curly brown hair. I was nine years old when she was born. I remember that day very well. She was born in early March during a major blizzard-like snowstorm. I remember that my mother was sitting at the kitchen table and she had her eyes focused on the clock in front of her. Later I understood that she was timing her labor pains. My father walked us to my Aunt Annie's house, which was about six blocks way. We struggled through deep mounds of snow to keep ourselves grounded. I remember that even my father kept slipping on the freezing terrain.

I think that nine years old is about the time that little girls begin to think of being mommies themselves. I often pretended to myself that Arlene was my baby. I know that I often took her for walks in her carriage. I even thought, quite proudly, that I was a better mommy than her "real" mom. I'm sure that my mother was grateful for the help and encouraged my fantasy.

I left for the convent when Arlene was nine years old. Our family visits were very restricted at that time, and so I did not experience any of Arlene's adolescent years. She has always seemed to me to be closer to my sister Frances and my brother Billy. Of course, that makes sense. As adults we often spend some vacation time together each year. However, we are not for each other, the friend that you might phone to go out to lunch or to go shopping. I believe that after I entered the convent there was some idealization of me by my parents and that was a source of irritation for my siblings. Although not my fault, or theirs, it has left some emotional limitations in the relationships and maybe some distrust.

The fifth child, Kevin, was born while I was in the novitiate. He is nineteen years younger than I. I have been told by my other siblings that when my mother discovered that she was pregnant with Kevin she said, "God took one of my children and gave me another." Kevin and I never lived together. When he was born, I was told by many that he looked enough like me to be my son. Although, of course, I love him, we never really had a relationship. Early in his adult life, efforts on my part to develop that relationship through some sisterly counseling resulted in an unfortunate misunderstanding which was never resolved. We certainly continue to care for each other, but the absence of truly knowing each other has created an underlying superficiality.

During these years there was another significant person in my life. She was my mother's sister and my Auntie Annie. I believe that she began to play an important role in my life after my sister Frances' birth. I'm sure that initially it was to help my mother who had two babies under one year old.

She and her family called me "Dutchie," because they said that in my early efforts to communicate, I sounded like I was speaking Dutch. I was very close to my Aunt Annie. I felt completely and unconditionally loved by her. She lived a very simple and uncomplicated life. I felt very safe with her. I spent many of my childhood weekends and vacations with her. She worked in a factory near my home, and I remember sitting on my porch steps waiting for her to pass our house so that I could wave as she walked home from work. In time my devotion and love for Aunt Annie did create a bit of jealousy on the part of my mother. I do now understand that.

4
Turbulent Weather

David R. Hawkins has said: "Spiritual work is a tremendous threat to the narcissistic core of the ego. Why? Because the ego believes that it is the source and core of your life. It does not give up without a struggle." He continues, "The ego must die itself. It is not an easy death." An appropriate metaphor for the ego was used by Jesus when he said, "The grain of wheat must fall into the ground and die before it can truly live." The grain of wheat represents whatever it is that stands in the way of our living authentic lives.

It has been a long and often painful journey for me to uncover and discover the false self, i.e., eagle complex, that I created even from childhood. I say that without any desire to be unfairly critical or judgmental of myself or of anyone else. I've often heard people who have gone through very serious bouts with cancer say that they now look back on it as a gift – a gift that has empowered and transformed them. As I continue to walk the walk I know that to be true.

I am reminded of the words of Rumi, a thirteenth century Persian mystic:

"Why, says the rose, "should a thorn sadden me,
When I grew this laugh because of a thorn?"

As I reflect on my desire to share my journey, I am surprised that it has taken this course. I know only that it has evolved in spurts of grace, supported and recognized by the wisdom people in my life.

Shortly after my eighteenth birthday I entered the convent. It was something that I had thought about especially in my senior year of high school. I had a very dear friend who entered the same community after our sophomore year. I visited her as frequently as possible and got to know the sisters. I was touched by their warmth and openness. I entered in the fall of that year. I don't know that I was a particularly religious teenager. I did the usual Mass on Sunday, Confession, and First Friday devotions. Interestingly enough, what I remember most about the intensity of my prayer happened when I was a child. I would lay awake in my bed and pray for hours that there wouldn't be "hell to pay" when my parents arrived home from an evening of celebration. Of all the things that I might remember that one is ingrained in my mind.

I also remember that as a young girl I daily took a short cut through the parish church on my way home for lunch. I repeated the same ritual on my way back to school. There was an oblong frame on the marble altar with a prayer written on it. I quickly said the prayer and went on my way. As an adult I often wondered what that prayer said. I had the opportunity to go back to that church and was surprised to discover that it was "A Prayer For Religious Vocations." God's ways are indeed mysterious!

I wonder if my desire to become a woman religious didn't, initially at least, support my "eagle complex." It certainly was a time when we were set apart and maybe set up to appear to be otherworldly. The religious habit itself created a framework for that.

I really grew up during those novitiate years. They certainly were not easy, but they carved out a container for me to begin to know and love God and others in deeper and more genuine ways. It was also a time when I came face to face with the limitations and burdens of the false self. I struggled and often lost the battle. However, for the first time I became aware of the work that needed to be done. Little did I know then that it was only the beginning of the challenges which I know now are the work of a lifetime.

After I took first vows I taught the first grade for ten years in a parish school. I loved it! I think that it satisfied my maternal instincts at that time. I also received a lot of love and felt very successful. Some years later I was having breakfast with a friend in a restaurant and I noticed a man who kept staring at me. I was no longer in the religious habit. He finally came over to me and asked my name. He then said, "You taught me in the first grade. I was so in love with you. I thought that you were so beautiful!"

Another time a friend of mine who taught French in College told me that she had asked her students to write an essay in French about a person who had made a difference in their lives. One young lady wrote about her first-grade teacher. She said that she remembered, "that her teacher was always present to each of her students." My friend, knowing that this student had gone to one of our schools, asked the young lady who she had written about, and she named me. It delighted me to know that I had made a difference. What I know now, and didn't know then, is that it was the "sparrow" in me that touched others. I will say more about that later. I share this because I believe that at that time "the sparrow" had found a home.

Unfortunately, after teaching the first grade for ten years I was asked to fulfill a need for a French teacher in one of our high schools. I did not major in French, but I had done very well in my high school and college classes. However, it didn't take long for me to realize that I was in over my head. I taught French 1,2, and 3. I barely managed to keep one page ahead of my students. I also taught English and Religion and was in charge of the yearbook. Those were the days! The contented little "sparrow" had to reach beyond her comfort zone and abilities and "pretend" to be an "eagle." I remember that in those days the sisters who were chosen to teach in the high schools were often seen as special. I ate it up!

After two years of teaching in the high school, I was invited by a friend and teacher in the school to investigate the possibility of applying for the position of Director of Religious Education in his parish. I had always had a special interest in religious education and spirituality, so I took advantage of the opportunity. I was hired and became one of the first Directors of Religious Education in the diocese. I was responsible for preschool through high school education in a very large parish. My job description also involved preparing parents to assist in the sacramental preparation of their children. This was new in the diocese and often met with resistance from parents who believed that this was the responsibility of the Catholic School and the Church. Once again, I was in over my head!

These were the years when life in communities of women religious, and in the Church itself, was going through many significant changes. Vatican II had a powerful and profound effect on many and in particular on religious communities of women. Many were re-evaluating commitments to religious life that they made as teenagers. I was one of them. I began to believe that I could do the ministry that I was doing within the Church as a lay woman. I also allowed myself to be in touch with my latent desire to be a mother.

I had spent more than a decade of my young adult life in a religious community. I must say that for the most part I received a lot more than I gave. I left with a grateful heart. I know that those years afforded me opportunities for growth and experience beyond what I might have imagined. I did continue to be in ministry with the Church as I had hoped.

5
Homing Time for the Sparrow

At Christmas time that year I was invited to the birthday party of a friend. While there I met the person, who within six months, was to become my husband. I think now that I fell in love with a projection of myself – not a healthy one. We closely shared the emotional limitations of our childhood families. I think that we both tried hard to fix the wounds in ourselves and in each other through this relationship, but it was beyond our capacity to do so at the time. We were both very good people with very deep scars. I believe that we did our best.

I mentioned that I had a strong desire to be a mother. When we didn't get pregnant within a year, we decided to give another child a family and a home. Joe was three years old when we first took him as a foster child. I became pregnant seven months later and Scott was born nine months later. Without a doubt it was one of the happiest times in my life. Soon after Scott's birth, Joe became available for adoption, and so we became a family of four. When Scott was about a year old, I became pregnant with our third son. It was a very exciting time. We were also moving into our first home.

My pregnancy with Sean was very special and intimate. Early in the pregnancy I found a small book in the book rack in the front of our parish Church. It contained a Scripture meditation and suggestions for dialogue with your unborn child. I prayed with it daily and as a result felt a special closeness with my unborn son.

When I was told, after his birth, that Sean was having difficulty breathing, I spent the whole day and night begging God to heal him. I repeatedly called on every place in Scripture that spoke of God's faithfulness – "If you ask the Father anything in my name, it will be given to you" – "Ask and you shall receive" – and many others.

When Sean died the following morning my grief raised desperate questions, "Why me? Why this? Where were you God when my son died?" I desperately tried to hold on to what I knew in my head – what I read and prayed in the Scriptures; yet feeling at the same time that I could never gaze on my God in the same way.

About this same time a very good priest friend of mine, asked, "May I share with you my belief about this? Of course, I said "yes" – my heart was broken, and I was looking for any kind of relief. He continued, "I believe that at the beginning of time God set this world into motion and because God gave us the gift of choice the world continues to evolve in a natural way." He continued, "I don't believe that God is responsible for Sean's illness leading to his death."

I experienced a physical and spiritual healing as I took in his words. I felt as if a huge boulder had been lifted from my shoulders. Of course, God didn't "do this" to my son. Sean was born with physical problems because we humans have created pollution and disease on our planet by the many chemicals and wastes that we have put into our environment. As a result, children are born with birth defects and, others both young and old, die unnecessarily, due to our disrespect and disregard for the health of our planet.

Is God faithful? Yes, God is faithful. How? God is intrinsically and extrinsically present to us in the very depth of our pain. God continues to embrace us with unconditional love and healing so that we can survive and even thrive as our lives continue to unfold.

That happened almost forty years ago. Following that, there was a radical shift in my consciousness and in my prayer. In my grief I missed the true meaning of the Scripture readings that I had prayed so desperately. As my personal experience of God's presence continued to evolve, I knew that God is not out there somewhere patting me on the back and assuring me that "it's all going to be O.K." Often it's not O.K. from a human point of view. God's presence is much more intimate than the often-unspoken belief that God is out there directing my life, and I am here waiting for direction. We are one with Divine Mystery and as such are co-creators of the path on which we travel.

After Sean's death life continued but it was never quite the same. I threw myself into my work in an effort to find relief from my loss. My husband and I seemed to handle it very differently. Communication became more and more difficult. We tried marriage counseling, but things didn't change very much. I was reading Scott Peck's book, *The Road Less Traveled* when, after a very tense visit on New Year's Day with my parents, I suggested a separation. The next couple of months were terribly difficult. I finally left the house and moved to an apartment with my two boys. They spent the week with me and weekends with him. He was a good father, and I believe he did his best for them.

6
The Eagle Soars

On Saturday, shortly after that, my friend Susie and I had plans to go to Neumann College for a talk being given by Robert Wicks, author, lecturer, and Chairman of the Graduate Pastoral Counseling Program at the college. When Susie phoned me to make plans to pick me up I told her that I wasn't going. She insisted on knowing why, and I finally told her that I had been crying all morning. That wasn't an acceptable reason for her, so she told me that she would pick me up in a half hour. I credit Susie with changing the trajectory of my life in a major way. After a most hopeful and uplifting lecture, Robert Wicks talked about the new Graduate Pastoral Counseling Program at Neumann. I was filled with enthusiasm! I went up to him and said, "I want to be part of that program, but I don't have any money." He said, "If you really want it there's always a way to get money."

He was right! The following Monday I called the bank to ask about getting a student loan. I remember speaking to a lovely lady who encouraged and supported my new vision. I soon had a loan for $10,000. At the time I was making $18,000 a year working as Director of Religious Education in a parish plus $800 a month child support, but I never missed a payment on the loan.

I went to two evening classes once a week. It was difficult, but I loved every minute of it. The faculty and adult students became a community. Much was expected of us, but much was given in terms of support. There was a lot of reading and papers to write. I used to get up very early in the morning before my sons got up for school to do my homework. We were also expected to maintain a practicum under the supervision of a licensed therapist. It became such a healing experience for me. Much of the confidence that I had lost over the past few years was restored. In retrospect I realize that the journey toward self-awareness and self-realization was about to begin.

During this time the decision was made for the boys and me to move back into the house. It was so exciting to reconnect with my neighbors and friends. I was still working in the parish and going to school at night, so the move took energy that was already maximized. As a result, I ended up with pneumonia and had to be hospitalized. It was weeks before graduation and the time when we were expected to write and present our exit papers. I was sure that I would have to wait until the next year to graduate. However, the staff assured me that they would find a way to review my paper and have me present it before graduation. And they did!

Graduation was wonderful! The "eagle" had new wings, but the "sparrow" was in the shadows. I decided to give myself a party and friends and relatives helped me do it.

We were not given "placement" options, so it was up to each of us to find a ministry in which we could work. I began working at a Lutheran ministry in which I had done some of my practicum. Shortly after that a psychologist in the area heard about my work and invited me to become her psychological assistant. The office was located in the middle of an area with a lot of crime. After having my office door thrown open a couple of times by a policeman, with gun drawn, looking for someone who had just robbed the liquor store on the corner, I decided to look for another place.

I had a friend who worked with a group of therapists in a beautiful new building on the edge of a lovely river surrounded by all that nature could offer. She and her group invited me to join them. She was a psychologist and the others were clinical social workers. I mention that because I had recently received a master's degree in pastoral counseling. Once again, the "eagle" was spreading her wings – one might say beyond her capacity to fly. I was however in supervision with the psychologist in the group. They were a lovely group of people, and I never felt less than a peer.

Unfortunately, after a couple of years it was discovered that the building was infested with dangerous mold. The building had won many prizes for its beautiful design – one of which was the ornate windows that could not be opened for fresh air. The entire building was airconditioned. As a result, many of us were dealing with sinus and breathing problems. I happened to be one of them. After the discovery of the mold we had to move out. There was some talk of litigations for recovery of medical and work-related issues, but I was not part of that.

So, this "eagle" was out and about looking for another nest. I soon joined a friend who had an extra office in a suite that she owned. It was quite small, but I was certainly grateful for her generosity.

I should mention here that since I was not working in a counseling center where often clients are referred by the center itself, I was responsible for my own referrals. I am still amazed that I was able to make a living without certain resources. It is usually very difficult to do that. Yet they came – some from other therapists and others by word of mouth. I was very fortunate and very blessed. There were also a couple of doctors who were especially generous in sending me referrals. Again, in retrospect I believe that the gifts in myself that I dismissed or easily disregarded, i.e., those of the sparrow, were the very ones that carried me forward in my work.

During this time the religious community to which I belonged decided to explore the possibility of associate membership for lay women and men who desired to share in a special way, our charism of peace through justice. I was very excited about this possibility and happy for the invitation to be a member of the committee charged with doing this. After a year of gathering information about what this might look like, we presented it to the next Congregation Chapter and it was approved for experimentation. I immediately wrote a letter to the Province Leader asking to be considered for membership and actually became the first to do so.

Associates are lay women and men who do not take religious vows but who do make a promise or covenant to live the charism of peace and justice in their daily lives. I was later asked to be the co-director of the associate program and did so for four and a half years.

It was also about this time that I was introduced to the practice of Zen. Two of our Sisters who eventually became Zen teachers invited me to sit with them in meditation. I think that I took to it like a duck to water. That's not to say that the practice is or was easy, but it afforded me a new and deeper pathway to self-knowledge and spiritual growth. I am reminded of Jesus' words: "by its fruit you will know it." Without a doubt the daily practice of Zen or "sitting meditation" has been the most informative and transformative blessing in my life. I have been able to experience and recognize its fruits – not the least of which is the ability to explore and share my struggle between the false self (eagle) and the true self (sparrow).

Another blessing that had a tremendous impact on my journey was that I was introduced to Sister Liz. She was the Diocesan Vicar for Women Religious at that time. She not only became my spiritual director, but she was directly involved in the discernment process that had just begun to percolate in my consciousness. She also invited me to be a member of a Spiritual Direction group that began to meet monthly. We met regularly for many years. As I reflect on this ongoing and progressive impact on my life – my knowing of myself and my relationship with God – I view my relationship with Liz, as well as with the women in those groups, as a blessing far beyond what I could have imagined. There is no doubt that who I am today was generously and wisely nurtured by and through them.

I was also invited to take advantage of a scholarship that was being offered to twelve members of the diocese for graduate study in Spiritual Direction at Neumann University. It meant another three years of evening classes, written papers, supervision, and a practicum. Of course, I accepted! Once again, I was grateful for the opportunity it provided for learning and a deepening communal experience.

For the sake of clarification this was while I continued to raise my sons, make a living, and maintain other commitments previously made. All are choices that I made and for which I take responsibility. I say this only to further point out what I now know as the "eagle complex."

Also, about this time, Margie, a very special friend of mine had an unexpected and tragic stroke. I went to visit her frequently in the hospital. During one of these visits another friend and I were on the elevator on our way to lunch. She reminded me of my long time wish to open a center of prayer for women. She asked me if I was still interested in doing that. I told her that I was but that I was no closer to a plan than I had been the last time that we talked. She then shared with me that she and her husband had had some good fortune recently and that maybe they could help. She also shared that this thought had come to her as a result of a retreat that she had participated in recently. There in the cafeteria of the hospital Spirit Center was born!

The "eagle" was soaring! Within a very short time we gathered a group of people, men and women, who we thought might be willing to help us. My friend and her husband provided some finances so that we could get started. The first thing that we did was to have materials professionally printed so that we could begin to advertise.

We heard that the diocese was sponsoring a special day for women on a certain Saturday, so we made it our first goal to set up a table at the gathering and to spread out our newly printed materials. We went to great lengths to decorate the table and even had a banner made. We had a drawing for anyone who came to the table and entered their information in the box provided. We were a big hit! Women were excited about Spirit Center. However, when they asked us where it was located we had to tell them that we didn't know – we didn't yet have a place.

Now this is how the magic happened! On the following Monday I went to my small office in my friend's suite, and there was a message on my phone from the man who owned the building. He said: "There is a suite on the second floor. I lived there for a short time while the building was being built and I was wondering if you might be interested in it? It's decorated and in very good condition. I would let you rent it for a modest price."

Are you kidding me? I didn't even know this man except to nod "hello" when I went in and out of the building. The suite consisted of a large entry room, two large offices, a large group room and a bathroom. What an unexpected answer to prayer! After that things just fell into place quickly.

We established a Board of Directors comprised of women and men from different professions and with different skill sets. They were invaluable, and we quickly became good friends. We had a lot to learn, but we met monthly and made it happen. I moved my counseling and spiritual direction practice into one of the offices and Margie (who initially offered her help) became the Office Administrator and used the second office.

We created a library consisting mostly of books about women's issues. We offered workshops for women and invited presenters from the area. Once a year we had a fun night for women. It was called "Women's Night Out." We had a speaker, refreshments, and gave out many door prizes. We even invited young women from the university to teach us some of the new dance steps. We also had a fashion show in which the board members and staff modeled clothing from a popular department store. It was a wonderful way to create community.

The establishment of Spirit Center certainly put me into the "eagle" sphere. However, I know that I have many people to be grateful to, for, without their presence and constant support, it would not have been a reality. My people skills badly needed the professional skills of those who knew how to run a business.

I also started to be a director on retreats at our community's and other retreat centers. It was a wonderful opportunity and privilege to companion women and men who were looking for deeper relationships with God. I received so much as I witnessed the love and power of God's Spirit in the transformation of each retreatant. I was reminded again and again that God is never outdone in generosity.

By this time my sons were young adults and were planning their own futures. Both of them were successfully employed and had met young women who would soon become their wives. Within a short time, both of them gifted me with three wonderful grandchildren. They are a blessing that is immeasurable and continue to bring much joy to my life.

7
Flying Full Circle

Soon after, I began to wonder about the possibility of going full circle and returning to religious life. I revealed this stirring in my heart first to my spiritual director, Sister Liz. I really can't pinpoint how this desire began to arise in my mind and heart, and I had no idea whether this was something that was possible. I do believe that God reveals God's Self in mysterious ways. The impact of my desire became quite apparent as I was walking along the beach with the sister who had recently been elected Congregational Leader. As I shared with her my desire I began to cry. She listened and suggested that we plan a weekend together so that we could discuss it further. We did, and with her support, she suggested that I meet with our Province Leader. I did that and again received support to move forward with plans to re-enter the community. I met frequently with my spiritual director who played no small part in my year of discernment. With her guidance and support I explored the mystery of God's newest movement in my life.

After a year of living part-time in community and taking courses to update my understanding of the vows, I wrote to the Congregation leadership asking to profess temporary vows. My request was granted and on November 11,1997 I took temporary vows for three years. My sons, their wives, and my only grandchild, at the time, attended the liturgy. I gave the reflection during the Mass and called it, "My Dance With God." I wanted to say that God was part of the whole journey (the dance). I do not believe that any single part was more important than the other. In some ways it was "a road less traveled" but in all ways it was an expression of God's continual walk with me.

I am reminded of Rumi's beautiful poem, "Giving Up Your Soul":

"Dancing is not rising to your feet painlessly like a whirl of dust blown about by the wind. Dancing is when you rise above both worlds, tearing your heart to pieces and giving up your soul."

- Jalal-ud-Din-Rumi

Sometime before I took my vows I remember a sister friend asking me, "If the community had a need for your help and your sons had a need for your help, which would you choose?" I said without hesitation, "I would help my sons because the community can always find someone else to fill their need, but my sons have only one mother." After twenty years I still believe that. I try to see my life as a whole and not as a division of lifestyles, and so I would go where the need is greater. I am fortunate that this has never been, nor do I expect it to be, a problem with my community.

Three years after taking temporary vows I asked for and received permission to take final vows.

On account of my already well-established ministries in Delaware, it was decided that I would remain there even though we do not have community residences there. I wanted, however, to live with a community of women religious, so I asked the Benedictine Sisters if I could join them. They graciously offered me a home. Once again it was a God-inspired choice. My years with them were blessed in many ways. We shared what was common to all of us – prayer, daily chores, joys, and yes, even many tears at the untimely death of our dear Sister Mary Paul, OSB.

While living with the Benedictines I continued my ministry at Spirit Center – the center for women. About six years into that ministry my religious community began to look for a Novice Director who would be asked to assist in the establishment of a Congregation Novitiate. I was asked to think about taking on that position.

One of the significant things that I remember in my interview with the Congregational Council was that I said, "I felt like a sparrow in a sky full of eagles." No one challenged that at the time, but in retrospect, I wish that someone had. It seems to me now to have been an unconscious warning of things to come. Although I had some reservations, I agreed to take on that responsibility. I spent the summer, with others, preparing the house for the arrival of the novices. I soon found out that that was probably the easiest part of the job.

When I accepted the position I prayed, "God, please help me to learn in this position what I need to know about myself." We've all heard it said, "Be careful what you pray for." God answered that prayer with multitudes of opportunities for self-reflection tinted with much pain.

For me it was a blessing disguised in many of the misconceptions that I carried about myself and others, probably from childhood. My knowing of who I was, was challenged on many levels. The recognition of my limitations opened many painful wounds from the past. The sense of failure that I experienced brought me to my knees and to the floor in the chapel many nights after everyone had gone to bed.

When I was finally relieved of the position, I cried all of the way down the turnpike back to Delaware. I cried, not because I was relieved of the position, but because Humpty Dumpty had finally fallen off the wall and I wasn't sure that she could be put back together again. So much of the false self that had supported me for so long was in a pile on the floor.

Except for the death of my son, I had never felt such sadness. I kept saying to myself, "But I did my best." And I did! But it wasn't enough. Believing that I was not enough was a very old wound in my soul. But I had to tumble under its weight in order to be able to name it and recognize its insidious nature.

I returned to my home with the Benedictines. It was such a wonderful place of love, healing and support. I renewed my friendships in Delaware and began to look for a place to start my spiritual direction and pastoral counseling practice again. I found an office close to the University of Delaware.

8
Eagle Eyed

What I began to suspect was that God's response when I prayed, "Teach me what I need to know about myself" was now pregnant with possibilities. At this time, I was also involved as a spiritual director on silent weeklong retreats at our community retreat center and at other retreat centers. This ministry brought me a renewed sense of meaning and compassion and invited me to greater clarity about my journey as well as that of others. As a "wounded healer" I had the privilege of being a companion to others as they sought to know more deeply God's love and desires for them. Of course, the gift for me was the overflow of God's grace as I become more aware of the places within me that needed healing.

"And once the storm is over, you won't remember how you made it through, how you managed to survive. You won't even be sure, whether the storm is really over. But one thing is certain. When you come out of the storm, you won't be the same person who walked in. That's what this storm's all about."

(Haruki Murakami)

We have all heard that God's ways are not always our ways. I don't know that I had any idea what I was asking for when I prayed to know myself better. It has not been an easy journey. I spent time whenever possible alone at a hermitage in Pennsylvania. I was once again blessed with the gift of a very skillful and loving spiritual director. It was in one of my meetings with her that I became aware of the metaphor of the eagle and the sparrow. It was one of those aha moments when you say to yourself "where did that come from?" It sounds silly now, but the realization and implications were very painful then. When I returned to the hermitage, I wrote and prayed:

A Retreat Plea

What is it that you desire of me, God asked,
What lies beneath your painful mask?

I wish I knew, I replied too fast.
I don't know, for what to ask.

Am I truly all alone? Have you gone too?
That thought brings grief and tears anew.

The loneliness and emptiness I fear
Are casting shadows everywhere.

Come, rescue me, my God, from such despair,
My only hope??? To know that you are near.

Self-awareness is the journey of a lifetime. Its course is often one step forward and two steps back. As I moved forward, I had to make friends with the eagle complex that I had adapted. Where did it begin? How did I feed it? What were the risks – the payoffs – the costs? And I had to befriend and celebrate the gifts of the sparrow.

"And you? When will you begin that long journey into yourself?" (Rumi).

Inspired by this invitation of the mystic and poet Rumi, I began to return to some of the resources that I had used years ago to understand the complexity of who I was. What I discovered was that time does give greater clarity to both understood and misunderstood images of ourselves. I don't know if that's actually the case or if age and hopefully wisdom, with God's grace, created a tension within that becomes impossible to ignore. Another mystery of God's love!

One of the resources that was especially valuable to me was the Myers-Briggs Type Indicator. It is a personality inventory based on the theory of psychological types described by Carl G. Jung for the purpose of making personality more understandable and useful in people's lives. It relies on basic differences in how individuals prefer to use their perception and judgment.

I discovered that according to this well-known and most widely administered personality test I scored INFJ – I (Introversion) N (Intuitive) F (Feeling) J (Judgment). According to what I have read this personality type is very rare, making up less than one percent of the population.

People with this personality type tend to have strong opinions, are strong-willed and decisive, act with sensitivity, imagination, conviction, and tend to see their purpose as helping others in life. They have a major need for time alone to decompress and recharge. They may tend to internalize conflict in their bodies and experience health problems when under a lot of stress. They are often found in service-oriented professions. They are not good at dealing with minutiae or very detailed tasks. They usually avoid such things or become so exasperated by the challenge that they fail to see the big picture.

I say: Yes! Yes! and Yes! to this brief and certainly incomplete assessment of the "self" that I have grown to know. I hasten to negate any impression that I might have given, that I am any more than a novice in my understanding of the complexities of this tool. However, it has helped me to name and recognize some of the features and gifts of this "self" for the purpose of self-knowledge and transformation.

What has this recognition to do with the journey of the eagle/sparrow? What choices did I make that created tension in the gut of the sparrow?

I believe that early in life I discovered that my sense of self depended on my ability to achieve and overachieve. Those were the ways in which I experienced acceptance and value. I internalized those messages to mean "You must make us proud." I think that I even believed that in doing that I could have an effect on the climate in my family life. That was a power that I rightly or wrongly assumed. As a result, I often made choices that were not in the best interest of my comfort zone and gifts.

How does that fit into the metaphor of the sparrow and the eagle? Well early in my writing I described the "sparrow" as "average / indistinguishable" and the "eagle" as "impressive / distinguishable." As a metaphor for "impressive / distinguishable" it makes sense to me that I chose the image of the eagle.

In doing so, however, I ignored the gifts and abilities of the sparrow. Nevertheless, I now "see" that these gifts were always operative on some level. I believe that they were the gifts that others saw in me and often acknowledged as important and valued by them. I am smiling as I recognize this reality. Perhaps that is a good sign, a sign that I am at last comfortable with the "me" that God chose to inhabit in human form.

There are no accidents as far as God is concerned. I have been given all that I need to be - all that God created me to be. What more can I ask for? "Sparrow" and "eagle" are merely metaphors that my ego and imagination created to teach me life lessons.

9
The Sparrow's Molting Instinct

Like any journey in life, the one toward spiritual transformation has many hills and valleys. The realization of the inner struggle between the prideful desires of the "eagle" and the acceptance of the "sparrow" has been rather recent.

As I begin to trace its pathways, I am reminded of something I wrote in my retreat journal on the evening of my recent birthday:

"I am grateful for all that has been given. My God has been very faithful. I have had many teachers and received from life many teachings. It has not always been easy, but I certainly have received all of the support that I needed to get me to this point." I continued: "My path has had a number of divergent twists and turns. Some complicated – some unexpected – some difficult. Some have resulted in great pain and others in great joy. Hopefully, I have been able to learn from most of them but I know that I am not finished. I am still here to be taught and to learn."

The knowledge of God's presence has been revealed to me throughout my journey – sometimes in very simple ways. I still smile as I remember a short poem that I wrote at the beginning of one of my hermitage retreats. It came to me through an invitation from my spiritual director in which she imagined Jesus' joy at having me to himself for the next few days. I entitled it:

"Goody Goody Said He"

"I got out of bed
And sat on the chair
Not yet aware that
Jesus was there.

"Goody, goody," said he
It's just you and me
No other distraction
Or useless interaction.

I'm ready and set
To give and to get
Today is a plus
Designed only for us."

What a wonderful gift to set me on the course for the rest of the week! I have found that writing is a way for me go to the depth of my inner self in order to name and feel what needs to be seen and felt in order to be healed and celebrated. Often it happens with great resistance and a lack of balance. As I noted before, the seductive impulse of the eagle continues to provide many opportunities for my ego to stray from my best intentions.

So many of the graces and insights that I have been given regarding this struggle come during the time that I spend at the hermitage.

There were certainly times when my retreat was an invitation from God to face some darkness and to dig deeper. Often when I tell people that I am going on retreat they say something like, "Oh, how wonderful." It's not always wonderful. Jesus said, "that we must die to ourselves." I believe that what he meant was that we need to face the parts of ourselves that get in the way of our being all that we are called to be. Some of those parts are almost as old as I am. Often that is painful, lonely, and even scary.

In a talk by Richard Rohr, renowned spiritual writer and lecturer, something that he said speaks to my understanding of the journey. He said that God allows opportunities for our egos to be disassembled in order for our true self to emerge. He asked his audience to think about the times in their lives when this was the case. I was able to name, without much difficulty, six major times. I chose heart-wrenching events that brought me to my knees and seriously altered my sense of self. The experiences also forced me to reexamine my understanding of God in ways that have been life changing.

St. Augustine reminds us that "we are travelers on a journey without as yet a fixed abode." We are pilgrims and daily we need to reflect on our fitness for the journey. "The journey is never done" advises Pope Francis, "Just as in each of our lives there is a need to restart, to rise again, to recover once again the goal of one's existence. "

One such new day at the hermitage I wrote:

A Morning Reflection

I got out of my bed
and opened the door,
What? - I thought -
does today have in store?

The woods were still dark,
The trees leaf and bark,
Providing an arc for
the morning's sun's spark.

Good morning I prayed
to these gifts of the earth
Today is a day
for newness and birth.

Creator of all - wonder you must
how wise it might be
to give and entrust
today's blessings to us.

"Pass them forward" I hear
as a response to my prayer
They are given to you
to love and to share.

Yes! This is the pact

that God gives to us,
Am I ready - today
or any day plus.

Will this evenings shadows
assure me of this,
Of what I've accomplished
or just what I've missed.

"Silly girl" responds my divine Sire,
You measure by mere human attire.
"I, says He, see below ego's mire,
Come, and rest in me,
to find love - worthy of desire."

10
Bird Song

There are those times when heaven and earth seem to meet in an expression of "meaning and knowing."

A Retreat Reflection

I am...
Sitting in a chair on the porch
Embraced and encapsulated
By the luscious green covering
Of earth.

I am...
Aware of the presence of Divine Mystery
Hidden in the spaces,
Between and above the trees.

I am...
Touched by the oneness of all,
And the reality of what is -
Whether known or unknown.

Pope Francis said that, "God is the Divine reminder of our worthiness." And of course, there are times in the presence of the Divine Healer when we are reminded of that. My personal experience of the presence of God continues to evolve. We are one in a mysterious but real way, and I am a co-creator with God on the path which I travel. Because we are human, we sometimes stray from that path. Fortunately, God's faithfulness does not depend on ours. In a recent Collect in the Mass we prayed to always revere and love God's name, "For you never deprive of your guidance those you set firm on your love."

"It is less about the journey and more about the One who beckons." Clare, my spiritual director, shared this with me on my recent Holy Week Retreat. It created a shift in my thinking. I went to the retreat primarily focused on the content of my recent story. You know – things like "who did what and when." What I was feeling about the latest "perceived" hurt.

What I realized from Clare's remark is that once again I was looking from the outside in – instead of the inside out. Retreats are sacred spaces to explore the mind of Christ, the God, who beckons us to heal not just from real or perceived everyday hurts. The Divine invitation is to reach a deeper place within that reminds us of who we really are and who it is who calls us. Certainly, during those retreats there are times when the sharing and exploring of ever-present hurts can become catalysts for a more grounded knowing of myself.

Perhaps I can more clearly relate it to the Paschal Mystery – life, death and resurrection – dying to the ego self and rising with and in the one true self – the Christ Self – the God Self.

Often, I am completely unaware of where God desires to lead me during those special days. It is not unusual for me to arrive with an unexpected heaviness in my heart. The miracle is that I always leave with a renewed spirit and greater insight.

My retreat reflections are for me authentic maps of the hidden treasures that my God has shared with me during those times. Sometimes I had to dig deep to find them. Sometimes they were aha moments that appeared spontaneously. Always they were worth the cost. As I made the choice to surrender and let go, they appeared in my writings as pathways to understanding and insight.

Letting Go - The Final Dance of the Autumn Leaves

I am sitting at the window in the hermitage
observing the Autumn leaves dancing
and swaying without inhibition
to the gentle urging of the light breeze.

They sway back and forth
finally settling beneath the trees,
the source of their daily nourishment.
released by Mother trees
to begin a new journey.
to become nourishment for the soil
on which they recently rested.

They let go without a struggle
in response to the whim of Spirit.
Too great a leap to suggest that She
who knows the number of hairs
on our heads knows also
the moment for each leaf
to leave Mother Tree? Perhaps not?

So many lessons to be learned -
The leaf children return to the earth
to prepare it to give birth
in the spring to another magnificent
and miraculous gift of God's
lovely imagination and generosity.

I pray for the freedom to let go
of what needs to die in me
so that like the leaves of Autumn
I too may become a source of life
and nourishment for others.

The gifts of creation that I have been privileged to share are often the catalyst for the reflection that follows – reflections that most often provide self-awareness and insight.

An Evening Prayer

Blessed are you, O God of the woods.
I listen and watch as your creatures become
more and more still.
In reverent movements they let
go of their daytime chatter.

The songs of the birds quietly bid good night,
and the chirping of the crickets becomes a mere hush.
The branches of the trees bow low to form
dark temples covering the fallen leaves.

I wonder where are the deer, the rabbits and the squirrels?
Stealthily and secretly they make
their way into the caverns of the earth
that they call home.
How easily these creatures embrace
the rituals of life.

The setting sun begins its journey to the other side
of the earth and
the harvest moon welcomes the stillness of the night.
Blessed are you Creator God of all that is -
Holy is your name!

In a biography of her life, author Joan Chittister, OSB says, "Every dimension of life, its gains and its losses, are reasons for celebrations because each of them brings us closer to wisdom and fullness of understanding." In *No Man Is An Island*, Thomas Merton, OCSO writes, "For when we are strong we are always much greater than the things that happen to us."

Once we are able to break through the certainties that keep us bonded to certain ways of seeing ourselves, we are free to welcome change and authenticity.

One of my favorite poems is one from the writings of Edwina Gateley:

Let Your God Love You

Be silent.
Be still.
Alone.
Empty
Before your God.
Say nothing.
Ask nothing.
Be silent.
Be still.
Let your God
Look upon you.
That is all.
God knows.
God understands.
God loves you
With an enormous love,
And only wants
To look upon you
With that love.
Quiet.
Still.
Be.
Let your – God love you.

So profound! So simple! Jesus invites us, "Come to me all you who labor and are heavily burdened and I will give you rest."

"I make no guess what greatness took me in.
I only know, and relish it as good,
that I am gathered more to God's embrace
the more I greet Him through my creaturehood."

These words from the poem, "Creature of God" by Jessica Powers, OCD express in a few words the power of transparency and authenticity before God. Being human is truly a paradox. An old Indian spiritual teacher might have expressed it best when he said, "The measure of enlightenment is how comfortable you feel with your own contradictions."

We know that we are called to the life of love and selflessness that Jesus modeled for us. Yet our imperfections and sinfulness remind us of our dependence on a God who loves us without conditions. A God who continues to desire deeper relationship with us – urging us always "to come as we are."

11

The Lark at Heaven's Gate

I have a great respect for my dreams. I think that they are channels for self-knowledge that arrive unbidden and often full of hidden treasures. I have had many dreams but two in particular seem to be significantly informative about my journey with the sparrow and the eagle. In one dream I was distressed about wet clothes on a clothesline because they had shrunk. In a second dream I was trying to find a bridal gown and in each shop the sales person brought me dresses that were ill-fitting and ugly. They were really not interested in finding me a dress. After some reflection, I realized that the message in these dreams was that what I was seeking (the wet clothes on the clothes line and the bridal dresses) were sources of distress for me because "they didn't fit." I was able to see these dreams' content symbolically representative of my unconscious drive to be an eagle. It "didn't fit." I am a sparrow and the gifts of the sparrow fit perfectly.

Self-awareness is the gift that keeps giving. It is the reality that we are given a lifetime of chances to realize what we were put here to learn. There is never a time when we can say "Now I have it all together." Often the struggle is the gift – not the deliverance from it. The prayer that I uttered at the beginning of my position of novice director became the catalyst for much growth and self-knowledge. Of course, I couldn't have imagined that at the time. The pain of that rejection brought to the fore years of struggling to be someone that I am not. I prayed, "God, help me to learn in this position what I need to know about myself". Wow! What was I thinking? We have heard the old adage, "Be careful what you pray for." It took a lot of support and time for me to unravel the meaning of that experience. I had to "let go" of the deep emotional baggage that I was carrying and begin to look "for the lesson to be learned."

Little did I know at that time that with the grace of God and the support of many that the metaphor of the eagle and the sparrow would emerge. It was a powerful insight and grace. It was the theme of so many of my choices and decisions. Do I still struggle with that at times? Of course, I do but more often than not, I now recognize its propensity, and I can look it in the eye and challenge its authenticity. There are lessons to be learned until we take our last breath and even then, I suspect that I will greet my God with an arm full of brokenness and unresolved ambition.

What a gift the eagle and the sparrow have been for me. They provided a context for me to understand with greater clarity who I am and how I can best serve God and others. Most importantly they helped me to name and appreciate the gifts that I have been given in order to participate more fully in the call that we have all been given to be our true selves.

12
A Bird's Eye's View

Many winter mornings I sat silently by the window in the dining room with a cup of coffee, focusing my attention on the old oak tree outside the window. It was very bare and its branches looked lifeless. They also looked dry and wrinkled. I thought, to many observers, this tree looks useless and maybe a little dangerous. I had heard of many such trees crumbling to the ground or hitting the roof of a house after some of the strong windstorms we experienced this winter. But not this tree!

I especially enjoyed looking through the bare branches of the tree and reflecting on the Cosmic energy – invisible to my eyes – but definitely sustaining the roots of that tree. I knew that the old oak tree wasn't dead. There was mysterious and intense activity happening in its roots – difficult for non-believers to see.

I started to love that tree and looked forward each morning to my visit with it. As spring approached the tree began to give birth to new buds. Not long after, it became plush with moist green leaves and a sparrow began to build a nest. What a miracle!

I also started to reflect on why this old oak tree touched me so deeply. What is it in my aging spirit that feels old and a bit lifeless? I am also wrinkled. At times my skin is dry.

Am I afraid that this makes me less visible to others? Less valued? Does the fact that I now walk more slowly make me useless and maybe a little too dangerous (to hold babies or keep up with the younger folk)? Yes, there have been some very strong winds – some self-imposed and some inflicted by others. Come to think of it – I share a lot with the old oak tree! But that's not the end of the old oak tree's story and neither is it of mine.

I, too, am supported and renewed by the presence of Mystery within me. Often not seen – sometimes not appreciated. In spite of that – "Mystery" continues to call me deeper and deeper into union with the Ground of all Being who promised this sparrow, "I will be with you always."

May the lessons of the old oak tree renew my commitment "to let go" of my desire to change the way things are and instead to celebrate the gift of all that is!

> "It is good to have an end to the journey,
> but it is the journey that matters in the end."
> Ernest Hemingway

References

Gateley, Edwina. "Let Your God Love You." In *In God's Womb: A Spiritual Memoir*, 59-60. Maryknoll, New York: Orbis Books, 2009. Used with permission.

Powers, Jessica. "The Legend of the Sparrow (For a child who dreams of sainthood)." In *The Selected Poetry of Jessica Powers*, 4-5. Washington, DC: ICS Publications, 1999. Used with permission.